Personal Finance:

7 Steps to Effective Budgeting and Money Management to Build Personal Wealth

By

Richard Stanton

2nd Edition

Table of Contents

Introduction

The secret to improve your personal finances and financial well being is by exactly knowing what your money is doing and where is it going. One of the best ways to keep track of your money is to create a simple budget, which has your earning, and spending put together in a sheet. Then comes the interesting part of how manage your money and how to grow it if you have identified the secret of saving.

This book will unfold a stepwise process for you to understand how budgeting is done at a simple level and how you can manage your money going forward. The book also unveils wealth management strategies that one can follow with ease. The step wise approach covers every topic in detail and elaborates all the doubts you had till date.

It will be an eye opener for you as you will understand your financial status clearly and what has to be done if you have a financial constraint. The book is covered for people who are in dire states and for someone who wants to manage their money well. After reading this book, you will be able to visualize what is essential for you, what is not so important for you and where are the areas clearly that you could save some money.

The popular myth is that wealth management is only for the rich and for people who have a great lifestyle. You will now understand that, once you get into the habit of saving you should know how you want your money to grow. You could opt for simple ideas of investing your money, because your friend said so or someone suggested you a better investing opportunity. This book will enable you to look at a holistic professional perspective of wealth management and what it means to you.

Step 1: Understand The Popular Myths Of Budgeting

The first impression anyone would have about budgeting is that it is a tiresome exercise and consumes lot of time. In the initial stages of planning and creating a budget, it may be time consuming and complicated but going forward it will have huge benefits. The hard work that is done in the initial days would not go waste, as you are able to see results before you.

Another general misunderstanding is that personal budgeting is only beneficial for individuals who are in dire financial circumstances. The fact is that even though personal budgeting can be an actual tool for people who face financial problems, it is also an exceptional tool for all others who want to keep their finances planned and in control.

Preparing a budget doesn't mean you can't spend

Apart from viewing budgeting as a negative process, consider that creating an expenditure plan will *permit* you to spend your additional income in any way you like. Generating a budget doesn't essentially mean that you need to cut all that is fun from your life. While a household living on a strict month on month earnings would have the largest problem justifying spending on anything that isn't essential, the budgeting process itself could disclose occasions for unanticipated fun. Don't believe me? Give it a shot and you will know! But remember to not take it too casually as you will end up giving up on it, eventually.

You don't need an excel sheet expert or a mathematician

The numbers are the simplest things while developing a budget. If you are able to do addition, subtraction, and division to certain extent it means that, you can handle mathematics. It is tougher to take an authentic look at your spending and choose which areas can be condensed to improve savings. If the numbers hold you back from budgeting, you may look at using a free spreadsheet application to make your life easier. The benefit of an application is you have the option of observing your budget as a graphical representation, and most of the times visualization can be a great benefit.

If it is budget it needs to be strict – let us see

A budget that has scope for changes is more effective. The foundation of any budget should recommend amounts for certain spending types or recurring bills within a given time. It so happens that you cannot stay within 100% of the budget that you have prepared, life treats you differently in the practical sense. A budget with flexibility permits expense heads to derive from other monthly expense heads within that particular month. For instance, if you have to spend more on buying clothes one month because of sudden travel, you can transfer some of your money set aside for restaurants that month.

You can also allocate your budgeting surplus in an expense head at the end of one month to be available in that expense head during the following month. If this is a regular incidence, consider reviewing the budget to more precisely reflect your spending necessities. In fact, it is a rule for you to look back at your budget at the end of every month to see if you have followed it correctly. Don't think you will be able to get away with extra sending. You must develop a sense of responsibility and ensure that you are doing right by your budget. After all, your budget is what is helping you spend less and preventing you from emptying all your financial resources. So it is best if it is a bit strict and making you do the needful.

Budgeting is only for the rich – a myth and nothing else

If you don't have lot of earnings, or if your spending is presently beyond your means, budgeting is vital. It does not mean that people who spend a smaller amount than they earn should not make a budget. Even households with high incomes benefit from budgeting because it needs a truthful scrutiny of spending habits. There are almost always choices to save, earn, and invest more money. The procedure also helps families with an extra amount after saving and investing and to choose how they want to spend their additional cash. What's more, you will inspire your children to take it up as well. So start motivating them and give them a chance to do the right thing in terms of monetary savings.

People don't need budgets

This is one of the biggest myths that hound people. They think that budgets are mainly for companies and not people. But in reality, people need it more than companies do. Imagine going about your monthly spending without a proper budget to help you, will that not be a very difficult journey? A budget is meant to help you increase your wealth potential and will surely go a long way in allowing you to have a large wealthy empire set up for yourself. After all, isn't that the main aim for most people? To become rich and have enough money by the time they retire?

Budgets aren't for people with secure jobs

This is another myth that needs to be busted! People with great jobs earning thousands of dollars a month assume that budgets are not for them and that they are better off without any such restrictions. But in reality, a budget is meant to help people save money regardless of whether they earn in hundreds or in thousands. Your budget will allow you to track your spending and know where you can save money. So don't think you don't need a budget if you are earning more, everybody needs one and you are not exempt from it.

Budgeting is boring

This myth is extremely rampant. Most people think budgeting is a boring process. But in reality, budgeting is a very interesting and intriguing topic. It gives you the chance to prepare tables and fill in data and ultimately end up with a savings amount for yourself. Something that useful can never really be boring. You might feel like it is a herculean task to prepare one, at the very beginning but with time, you will realize that it is actually quite simple and can be done within a short amount of time. Don't take it too seriously and you will realize how interesting it really is to prepare a budget.

Budgeting is time consuming

The next myth states that preparing a budget takes a lot of time. But this is only a myth! If you have a ready-made table, then you can start filling in the data easily. How can that be time consuming? What's more, if you have all your papers and documents ready then it will be even easier for you. You will only have to read the data from it and fill it into the tables and you will have your budget ready in no time at all. So don't think of it as a time consuming process and do your best to shorten the time taken to prepare a budget.

Mental budget is best

Many people think that a mental budget is the best type of budget to prepare. But a mental budget will only confuse you and give you false hope. You will not have your budget ready for your easy reference, and will end up making mistakes. Besides, you will become just so busy with other things that you won't remember your mental budget after a week!

But it is a good thing if you are already making mental budgets, as you can easily put it on paper. All you have to do is spend a few minutes in writing down your mental budget, and your work will lessen considerably.

Tracking my spending is budgeting

This is one myth that prevents many people from preparing a monthly budget. Remember that your spending is just one half of your budget. A budget incorporates your earnings, spending, saving and debt repayment. So just by tracking your expenses you are not saving any money. You are only making it worse for yourself, as you will feel like spending more if you keep track of only your expenditure. Don't think you are budgeting by making note of your spending alone, and you have to sit down and seriously prepare a monthly budget for yourself, if you wish to be left with a substantial amount of savings at the end of the month.

My earnings differs so I can't prepare one

There is no such rule! It does not matter if you earn a certain amount this month and another one the next, your budget will be a reflection of your earnings and spending and so, the varying amounts are no reason to not prepare one! In fact, those with varying incomes must compulsorily prepare a budget, as compared to those with a consistent income. It will be easier for you to know how much money came to you in a particular month, and how you will allocate it. You will be happy with the outcome and in a great position to use your money wisely.

One needs to have debts to prepare a budget

It is a great idea to prepare a budget if you have debts, no doubt, but even if you don't, you still need to prepare a budget for yourself. It is better to start when you have no debts, as you can remain prepared when you actually do incur some. Even if you never do, you will have a good opportunity to save on a lot of money, and have enough, and more, for your retirement. You will also be debt free in no time at all, and start living the life of your dreams.

The same budget works for all

This is another popular myth that needs debunking. It states that one size fits all. But how can the same budget apply to everyone? It will obviously differ from person to person. It will depend on a lot of different factors including monthly income, spending habit, saving habit, debt repayment technique etc. So using the same budget format by borrowing it from someone is never the best idea. Learn to prepare your own budget format, and use it to prepare your budget. Through the course of this book, you will learn how to prepare a budget. You can take the basic format and tweak it for yourself.

Budgets means financial security

Finally, here is a myth that causes many people to not save

any money for themselves! It states that preparing a budget translates to financial security. But as you know, just preparing a budget does not mean financial security. In fact, it does not mean sure shot savings either. It is a mere tool that encourages you to save money on a monthly basis. It helps you understand the different ways in which you can increase your income and cut down on your spending, to remain with a big surplus at the end of the month. So don't assume a budget to spell financial security for you and fool yourself.

Budgeting doesn't have to be a routine. Add a customized method and find the one that works best for you. Contemplate that it is a plan for permitting rather than preventing spending.

Step 2: Net Income, Expenses And Budgeting

The next step in developing a personal budget is to know exactly what your net income is. The net income can be demarcated as the take home pay after all the taxes and deductions are subtracted. All extra incomes such as income from rentals, income generated from self-employment, income sources from interest/dividends, earning from child support/alimony and others should be included in the total net income calculation.

If you are not able to compute your net income due to lack of data, earning variations and other indecisions, do your best to guess and come up with a fair net income number.

The next step is to list and write down all your noticeable and hidden expenses and categorize them into the following four groups, which are Fixed, Flexible, Intermittent and Optional expenses. The most appropriate method of computing your monthly expenses is by studying your monthly purchase bills. If you have not saved your bills in the past, start collecting them in the future. This way, you could keep track of your spending to see where your money is going.

Fixed expenditure:

These expenditures occur month on month and the dollar

amount typically remains unaffected for longer durations of time. For example, rent, mortgage, childcare, premiums related to insurance and car monthly payments can all be categorized as fixed expenditure.

Flexible Expense:

This expenditure also occurs on a month on month basis, but the dollar amount often differs from one month to the other. Flexible expenditure comprise of expenses related to food, utilities, gas, household expenditure, payments related to credit card and so on.

Intermittent Expenditure:

This expenditure can be categorized as expenses that occur on a frequent, but not month on month basis. Some of these expenses comprise of insurance related to auto, medical, home and auto maintenance, memberships and premiums related to life insurance.

Optional Expenditure:

These expenses are classified as purchases that fall outside one's requirements. In simple words, it means luxuries of life that you can live without. Holidays, personal gifts, personal grooming and care, costly subscriptions and entertainment can all be recognized as optional expenditure.

Consider your income

The first one to consider is your paycheck. While you are aware that Uncle Sam gets his eye first on your hard-earned money, you may not be ready for how much the Government will take. For instance, if you earn a salary of $40,000 per annum, you'll likely only see about $32,500 (approximately) after deducting taxes related to federal, Social Security and Medicare governing policies. That may not include state taxes or any subtractions from your paycheck related to workplace benefits, such as medical policies and insurance pertaining to dental or a savings plan of your choice related to retirement. While all this is being discussed, you are likely looking at a net take-home pay of approximately $28,500 or so per annum. And this contributes to a net income of about $2,375 approximately per month.

Consider your expenses

Now you know what you could expect to take home. This will enable you to allocate portions in your paycheck. Here is an overall guide to help you budget your money to make sure your expenditures are covered. You may have to make some adjustments for your situation. If you spend less on your home, for instance, you can put the additional money from that category toward paying your debt. The dollar numbers within the brackets are based on our above case of a $40,000 gross salary with a monthly net take home pay of $2,375 per month after all deductions.

- 30% ($712) Housing
- 10% ($237) Utilities and other housing expenditures (including renters insurance)
- 15% ($356) Food (at home and away)
- 10% ($237) Transportation (including car loan)
- 10% ($237) Debt repayment (student loans and credit cards)
- 10% ($237) Saving
- 5% ($118) Clothing
- 5% ($118) Entertainment
- 5% ($118) Car insurance and miscellaneous personal expenses

In terms of dollar figures, this actually breaks down very close to the lines of what things will essentially cost you. Housing, of course, will vary subject on your location and also on whether you live unaccompanied or with roommates. Debt repayment is extra wild card for which you may have to make changes. But for now, let's take a micro view at the utilities and household expenses categorization.

Utilities

We start with utilities, primarily gas and electricity. Your actual cost may differ by the place you stay, season and how well your apartment is maintained. If you live in Nevada, for example, you may spend a lot more on air conditioning this summer than someone in Minnesota. But budgeting an average of $40 to $60 per month to power an air condition in two-bedroom apartment should be enough. Many apartments are inclusive of garbage and water service, so you may not need to worry about that.

Rent Insurance

For rent insurance, a hands on policy can be obtained for about $200 a year—or $17 a month.

Expenses related to Internet, Phone and Cable TV

You can save money on your Internet service by going back to the previous years of dial-up if your usage is minimal. You can still get a service for about $10 a month. But if that's too awkward for your lifestyle, consider getting fiber service through your Cable TV provider. You would usually get a discount deal for combining services together. The national average cost for basic cable is about $15 a month—$30 for next level, to which most of them subscribe. Add a fiber Internet connection for $40, and you are good to go with a budget $70 for the whole package.

You might save money on your phone bill by getting rid of your land line altogether and using your cell phone. (A typical landline service costs about $20 to $25 a month.) Cell phone bills could vary widely by location, provider and, of course, your own personal usage. But the normal cell phone bill in the U.S. runs about $40 to $60 a month. If that's too sharp for your budget, contemplate using a prepaid cell phone that charges you only for the minutes you use. If that's too conventional, you may have to look for other areas to cut back.

Add these to your total

Add them all - $40 for utilities, $17 for renter's insurance, $70 for cable and Internet plus $40 for your cell phone, and you're looking at $167 a month. We had budgeted $237, so that leaves you a $70 cushion for those months in which costs may vary. And if you live with a roommate, you may be able to share the cost of your utilities, cable and Web access, giving you even more leeway in your budget.

More Adjustments

The biggest areas to look out for are transportation and debt repayment categories.

Transportation: Look at the brighter side

If you own your car outright, $237 a month for transportation is a good estimate—or possibly even too high. But if you have a car loan, your monthly payment will probably be more than $237 to start with; apart from the money you'll spend on gas, parking, maintenance and repairs. So before you work out after graduation to buy your first car, make sure you are aware of the actual cost of buying a car. For maintenance and repairs, you should budget at least $500 a year, or $50 a month—maybe more if you're buying a second car.

For gas, let's assume you drive 1,000 miles a month and your car averages 25 miles per gallon. You'd need to budget $100 per month with prices at $2.50 per gallon. That leaves only $87 for a car payment, parking and other transportation expenses (approximately). This makes it really tough.

Some cities are easy to move without a car, thanks to well-organized public transportation and bike paths. But in other cities, a car becomes truly is a necessity. Try an option of carpooling with known people or coworkers. Or reduce somewhere else in your budget— like on food and entertainment or take on a roommate to divide the cost of rent to help make ends meet.

Groceries

It is easy for you to save on your groceries by choosing a store that allows you to use monthly coupons. These coupons can be used in exchange for groceries and every day necessities and you can save on a lot of money. These coupons can be cut out from newspapers or availed from online websites. There are hundreds of people who make use of this technique and get away with a 90 to 99% discount on their overall grocery and utility spending.

Styling and clothes

You can cut down on your clothes and styling spending by recycling your old clothes and styling at home by yourself. All you have to do is look up videos online and find some ways in which you can easily recycle your clothes. You must also look for ways in which you can cut your hair and do your nails. All of this will help you save on at least $100 a month, which can be directed towards your savings account.

Entertainment center

You can buy yourself a good entertainment center and use it to watch movies or sports. This will enable you to save on quite a bit of money. You can buy a second hand system if you like and use it to watch movies. You can also invite others over and have a good time. Ideally, you must save around $50 to $80 buy using this technique.

Homesteading

You can also choose to homestead if you think your monthly bills are skyrocketing. Homesteading refers to growing your own produce and also storing them for long-term use. You can save on a lot of money in a month by using this technique but must plan it out to avail its proper benefits. Make a list of all the vegetables and fruits that your family consumes in a month. Start growing them batch-by-batch and then store them by freezing, drying or dehydrating. If you get it right, then you can easily save up to $1500 a year. If you are left with a surplus then you can sell it online and make a little money as well!

Gift a service

Many times, we end up giving away expensive gifts to our friends and spend a lot of money. This can easily be avoided by gifting a service. This service can be anything that will be of use to the end user. People prefer to cook a meal or mow the lawn or wash the car. All these things will be of great use to the receiver and you will not have to spend a lot of money. But don't gift the same service repeatedly and change it up to introduce variety.

Buy off season

Another idea to save money is to buy gifts and cards when the holiday has passed. The goods will be much cheaper. Just make sure you don't buy something that mentions the year on it. You can buy it in bulk and store it in a safe place until next year.

How to Increase your Income On A Monthly Basis

As you saw in the previous section, there are many things that you can do to save on money, on a monthly basis. Right from cutting down on telephone bills to saving on gas money, there are several small things that a person can do in a month, to save a few dollars.

But saving money is not enough if you wish to increase your monthly income and plan for your retirement. Your salary will not always be enough for you, and you will need other types of incomes to supplement your monthly income.

In this section, we will look at the different things that you can do in a month to increase your monthly income.

Investments:

Making investments in the stock market or in a business is a good way to increase your monthly income. Here, you will have the chance to earn a regular income in the form of profits or dividends. You will not have to actively participate in the earning process and your money will work for you. We will look at investment options in detail in the next chapter.

Bank interest:

This is one of the most popular ways in which you can increase your monthly income. All banks encourage their customers to place a certain amount of money in their bank, on which they pay a certain interest. That interest will vary according to the saving and the more the investment the more the interest earned on it. So you can choose to place all your spare money in the bank and earn an extra income every month, based on your investment. It will be an easy thing to do, and will not involve your direct participation.

Rent:

The next thing to consider is availing rent on your property. This is a form of passive income that has earned itself great reputation. All you have to do is buy yourself a property and then rent it out. Even if you avail a loan for it, you will be left with extra rent money after paying for mortgage. You can kick back and relax and have the money role into your account without you having to sweat it out. You can also rent out a commercial establishment if you like.

Sales:

If you are good at cooking or making artifacts or handbags, you can sell them and make money. As and when you find spare time, you can make some and sell it, to earn a few extra dollars a month. If you work in an office then you will have a ready audience for your goods. You must expand your business and ensure that you are exploiting your full potential.

EBooks:

If you are good at writing stuff then you can write an eBook and put it on sale. You can also write a novel and find a publisher who will publish your book. But ensure that you make it as unique as possible, as there is a lot of competition out there. You can sell it online and every time someone downloads your book, you will earn a certain amount of money from it. You can choose to write one or multiple books based on your area of expertise, and interest in the subject matter.

Affiliate marketing:

Affiliate marketing refers to starting your own blog and then tying up with a company to promote their products. You must have a popular blog for this technique to work for you. It is important that you choose a topic that has a lot of readers, and will guarantee you a lot of hits. You can then approach companies and if they like your blog and number of visitors then thy will give you links to their website that you must sprinkle all over your blog. Every time someone buys from the site through your blog, the company will pay you for it. So this is a great option for you to try out.

Self help videos

You can also create videos and sell it. If you are good at something like helping people with software or explaining a math problem, then you can tape it and make cds out of it. You can then sell it online. When someone buys it, you get paid for it. Just like the eBooks, you can create as many cds as you like and use it to your advantage. But keep it simple and unique for people to like it.

Building apps:

You can build apps if you like. As you know, apps are all the rage these days and you can build some that are useful to others. You can sell it on some platform like an app store and every time someone downloads it, you get paid for it. Again, keep it unique and ensure that it provides good value to the end user. Don't stick with the old and outdated topics, and choose something that will help you create a niche market for yourself.

Hobbies:

There are many hobbies that you can capitalize upon and earn money using which. Say for example you are proficient at performing yoga poses. You can teach others yoga, and make money out of it. Similarly, if you have the hobby of collecting stamps or coins, then you can sell them, one by one, and earn some extra income from it. Another good idea is to indulge in gardening and sell the flowers and herbs that you grow. There are many such possibilities and you will only know their true worth, when you begin exploiting them.

As you can see, there is dearth of opportunities when it comes to increasing your monthly income and you can choose anything that you like.

Preparing a monthly budget

A budget is a blue print that you use to understand your monthly incomes and expenditures. So if you earn $2000 a month and spend $1000 then you are left with a surplus of $1000. Similarly, if you earn $2000 and spend $2500 then you are left with a deficit of $500. That deficit is your loss and it is important that you correct your budget.

In this section, we will look at the steps you must adopt to prepare your budget.

Step 1: prepare

The very first step to undertake is to prepare yourself, to formulate your budget. Collect all your salary statements, other incomes statements, bills, receipts etc. All of these are required for you to formulate your budget, and you must ensure that each and every slip is collected and assembled before you sit down to do the needful. If you have a spouse or a partner, then, collect theirs as well. It is best to have a hard copy of everything, as opposed to, a soft copy as you will know whether or not something has been accounted for.

Step 2: tables

The next thing to do is prepare the tables for your budget. Start by drawing out the basic outline and then divide it into 4 headings. The first one is named *Incomes* and the one next to it is *Income Amount* followed by *Expenses* and then *Expense Amount*. This is a very basic format for a budget and is used by several people worldwide owing to its ease in application. You can also choose the same and use it to formulate your budget.

Step 3: incomes

The first column to fill out is known as the incomes column. As you saw before, you will have incomes coming in through different sources including your salary, your portfolio investments, your passive incomes etc. All of these need to be recorded one after the other and their respective amounts mentioned next to their names. It is best to not round off any of the amounts and allow them to remain whole. You can also mention any remarks in brackets if you like or add in the statement's account number.

It is best to not add any intermittent charges, as they are temporary.

Step 4: expenses

The next column to fill out is known as the expenses column. The expenses column is where you add in all the expenses that you incur. This can be a monthly list of all the places where you pay money to avail products or services. We already had a look at the most common expenses that you might incur in a month, and you must also add in certain other incomes that are exclusive to you. Again, don't add in any intermittent expenses as they are not permanent in nature and will not occur consistently.

Step 5: surplus

Once you fill out all your incomes and expenses, you must check once more to see if they have been added in correctly. If it is correct then total the incomes column and then the expense column. Write down the total of the income first followed by the expense. If you are left with a positive value then that is your surplus. This surplus is your profit and that which you can invest wherever you like. Most people prefer to transfer it to their savings account but that choice is left to you.

Step 6: deficit

Remember that you might not always be left with a surplus. Once you tally your incomes and expenses, you might get a deficit, where your expenses are much higher than your incomes. That will cause you to remain with a deficit or a loss. But don't worry, as it is fine to have a loss. It just indicates that you are over spending and need to wise up. You can do so by cutting down on unnecessary expenses that you indulge in. your first goal will be to make the incomes and expense columns match and then start reducing the expenses further to create a surplus for yourself. Go through all your expenses keenly to see if there are any unnecessary expenses present. Remember that you might not identify them as being unnecessary if you don't think it through.

Step 7: short term savings

When you are left with a surplus, you must decide where to invest your money. One good idea is to divide the money and invest it in two different places. The first one being short-term investments and the other being long-term investments. Your short-term investments are those, which you use for your short-term goals. Say for example you wish to take a holiday in a year's time and tour the world. For that, you can add in around $300 to $500 a month. This short term goals differ from person to person and you must choose a substantial amount of money to transfer to the account on a monthly basis.

Step 8: long term savings

The next type of savings to consider is known as long term savings. This long-term savings is for the long run. Here, you must plan into the future and save for your retirement. How much you contribute towards this account is your choice. You can choose $500 or $1000 depending on your capacity. But don't worry if you are able to contribute only $20 or $30, as that is also a fair investment. Make sure you don't access the money in this account at any point in time even if there is an emergency. You can have a separate emergency fund if you like and use the money to pay for it.

Step 9: follow up

Following up on your budget is extremely important. If you don't, then you won't know whether or not you are on the right track. Go through the budget every now and then and check whether you are doing the right things. If you are over paying and your expenses are going over board then you must curb it and ensure that you save money on a monthly basis.

Step 10: separate budgets

It is best to maintain a separate budget for yourself and your spouse. If you mix them then there are chances of duplication. So maintain two different ones as it will be easier for both of you to refer to.

Sample budget (deficit)

Monthly Incomes		Monthly Expenses	
Monthly salary received	$1000.00	Rent paid	$300.00
Portfolio income received	$200.00	Creditors paid	$200.00
		Credit Card bills paid	$300.00
		Medicines bills paid	$40.00
		Gas bills paid	$100.00
		Food/Groceries bills paid	$60.00
		Singing Class fees	$60.00
		Personal Care expenses	$40.00
		Clothing expenses	$100.00
		Night out with friends	$300.00
Total Income	$1200.00	Total Payable	$1500.00
Total income	$1200.00		
(-) Total Expenses	$1500.00		
Deficit	$-300.00		

As you can see, here, there is a deficit at the end. This means that the person is over spending. But the budget can be tweaked a little and turned into a surplus budget. All you have to do is get rid of some of the unwanted expenses and adjust your budget.

Let us see how that can be done in the next tables.

Monthly Incomes		Monthly Expenses	
Monthly salary received	$1000.00	Rent paid	$300.00
Portfolio income received	$200.00	Creditors paid	$200.00
		Credit Card bills paid	$300.00
		Medicines bills paid	$20.00
		Gas bills paid	$100.00
		Food/Groceries bills paid	$60.00
		Singing Class fees	$00.00
		Personal Care expenses	$20.00
		Clothing expenses	$50.00
		Night out with friends	$0.00
Total Income	$1200.00	Total Payable	$1050.00
Total income	$1200.00		
(-) Total Expenses	$1050.00		
Deficit	$150.00		

Here, only a few changes were made in the table and the person is left with a surplus. Similarly, you must also tweak your budget to come into a profit for yourself.

Taking budgeting seriously

I know it will be difficult for you to take your budget seriously, especially at the very beginning. You will wonder if it is worth the effort, or you are better off without preparing yourself a budget. Here, you must understand that your budget will prevent you from over spending your precious money and leave you with enough for your retirement. So, yes! It is an extremely important part of your financial routine and you must prepare a budget without fail.

Here are some things to do when you prepare your budget.

Timing

The very first thing to do is, set an appropriate time to prepare your budget. The time has to be convenient for you and your family members as well. It is best to choose the hours before your office, as your mind will be fresh and you will not feel bored easily. It is best to spend at least 30 minutes to prepare your budget, and it can take longer if you wish to prepare a detailed budget. In order to remember to prepare your budget, time it with an activity that you perform regularly. It can be timing with a show that you watch on TV, or some such activity. Most people prefer to prepare their budget on the first day of the month but you can also prepare it on the last day as you will be prepared to sort out the expenses as soon as you receive your salary.

Place

Just like the time, you must choose an appropriate place for yourself. This place should never be in front of the television on your couch! It shouldn't be in your bedroom on your bed either! These places will distract you. So the best place to sit and prepare your budget is on a study desk. You can also choose the dining table, but make sure there is no food around you, as you will feel tempted to eat away! Choose a neutral place where you can sit and prepare your budget in peace.

Books

Buy yourself a journal and keep it safe. Buy a book that is easy to record in, and so, choose something that already has lines and tables meant for a budget. Buy yourself just one book and not too many. Make sure it is easy to carry around and not too heavy. A hardbound book is always a good option as compared to a flimsy book. But it is also a good option to choose a contemporary method like using an excel sheet, as there, you can easily create tables and fill in the details of your budget.

Software

There are many software that you can download and use for your budgeting. These softwares are available for download on the Internet and can also be downloaded from android and apple app stores. Some of the best budget softwares to use include "Acemoney" and "Moneystrands", both of which are easy to use and operate. You can download them and start using them immediately. They will lessen your work and you can easily maintain your budget for a long time. Retrieval will be that much easier as you can quickly open the app and look for whatever you are searching for.

Motivation

Motivation is vital when you wish to develop a permanent habit. So put in efforts to remain motivated, and prepare your budget without fail. During the first month, keep referring back to your budget several times to remain motivated. Once you realize that your budget has made your life easier, you will feel motivated to continue preparing it regularly. Your budget will also serve as a reminder of your financial progress, which will further motivate you.

Here are some things that you must not do when you wish to prepare your budget.

Distractions

The very first thing to not do is have distractions around you. It's not co incidence that you will feel like watching the television or head out and meet your friends or take a call, when you are preparing your budget. You must make up your mind to not get distracted by anything at all, and remain focused. Make sure there are no background sounds like the television or some such. You will feel distracted and decide to move away from your budgeting activity. So ensure that you are not easily disturbed by any of these unnecessary distractions when you are preparing your budget.

Impatience

Impatience is another vice that you must be wary of. Don't remain impatient and develop a high degree of patience. Pick yourself a time, when you are relaxed and are not feeling jumpy. So it is best to choose morning times after your shower or an hour in the evening after your work. Remain calm and composed and make use of a calculator to do all of the math in your budget.

Over dependence

Do not depend on anyone to remind you, to prepare your budget. You must prepare your own budget and not rely on another person to help you. If someone voluntarily decides to help you then well and good, but it is not thoroughly important. If you are preparing for your partner as well, then start with yours, and then prepare theirs. It is best to sit together and do it, so that discrepancies can be eliminated. Remain as independent as possible while preparing your budget to remain inspired.

Hiding expenses

It is important to not hide any expenses. Many people decide to hide certain expenses, which arise out of fulfilling are their guilty pleasures. You must not hide them and mention it in your budget. Instruct your spouse to do the same and not keep any expenses from you. Your budget is supposed to be as transparent as possible and not conceal anything.

Over expecting

Don't over expect from your budget. It is meant to help you save on money no doubt, but will not by itself transfer your money to your savings account. So don't kick back and relax just because you have prepared a budget. You must spring into action and do the needful to save your money on a monthly basis.

These are just some of the things that you must do and not do to take your budgeting seriously.

Plan for debt repayment

Regarding debt repayment, a college senior graduate at the time of graduation will at least have $20,000, on average, as student loan debt. If you fall into this category, you'll spend $230 a month approximately on a standard ten-year repayment schedule at 6.8 percent interest. You may need to negotiate a different time schedule with your lending bank, say, and a 15- or 20-year repayment. Or you can ask for a graduated repayment schedule where you pay less per month now, but more toward the end of your loan period. There is also an income contingent repayment, which bases your bill on a percentage of your actual salary.

The average college senior also will have an approximate $3,300 in credit card debt. At 18% interest and paying $80 a month (4 percent minimum payment of initial balance), it'll take you about two and a half years to rid yourself of that debt. And that's assuming you don't charge another dime

First option will be to pay for yourself

Try and stick with the fixed amount (or higher) in savings category. This is an outstanding habit to get into right from the word go.

Start by accumulating your short-term emergency savings, and then venture out into investments for the long term. If a 22-year-old saves $211 every month and earns an average annual rate of 8 percent on her money, h will have about $951,000 saved up by the time he turns 65. If he increases his monthly contribution every time he gets a raise, sticking with the 10 percent savings rule, he will have well over $1 million – perhaps even $2 million.

There is an exception to this rule, however. If you have high-interest debt, you would do better to take your 10% savings allotment and pay off your credit cards first and then start saving. It does not do any good to earn 8 percent on your savings if you are paying 18% on your credit card balance.

Debt repayment techniques

When it comes to debt repayment, there are two main techniques that people make use of. The first one being the snowball method and the second one being the avalanche; both of these are valid debt repayment techniques, and you can choose either one, depending on what your debts look like.

Let us look at both of these in detail and understand their individual pros and cons, which will help you, decide on the best one for yourself.

Snowball method

The first method to consider, to repay your debts is known as the snowball method. This method is quite popular, and is used by many people to repay all of their debts at the earliest.

As the name suggest, the snowball method makes use of the snowball concept. Just like how a small ball of snowball will roll down a slope and grow in size by collecting snow on its way, you will start with a small amount to repay, and then increase it as you go.

This technique is much preferred, as you have the chance to start with the smallest amount to repay, and then progress to a bigger one. You will have to write down all your debts in the ascending order and can also club two or more of the small debts together. The largest amount should be mentioned at the very end of your list. You can increase the amount as you go. It is believed that a majority of Americans favor this technique as compared to the other one, and rank it higher owing to its ease in application. But this technique is best suited for those that have many small loans and just one or two big ones.

Advantages

The main advantage of this technique is that, you will develop a strong sense of confidence and assurance, when you follow this method. Once you start repaying the debts, you will feel extremely light and know for sure that you have the capacity to repay your debts in full. This confidence will allow you to aim higher and be done with all your debts in no time at all. Apart from this, you also have the advantage of starting with a small amount, and not worry about raising a big sum to start repaying your debts. You can get done with all your small loans in express time, and can also club them together to make it easy for yourself.

Disadvantages

The main disadvantage of this technique is that, you will end up paying more than what you actually should be paying for your borrowings. This is because you will end up having heftier debts awaiting you, which will attract a lot of interest. So ultimately, you will have to take care of a big amount at the end, where your principle borrowing would have doubled or even tripled in value. The small amounts can be repaid anytime as they will not attract a big interest, but that is not the case with your big borrowings. This is the exact reason why many people don't opt for this technique of loan repayment and consider the next option for themselves.

Avalanche method

The avalanche method is the other debt repayment method that is used extensively. As the name suggests, this method operates like an avalanche. It starts off as a big mass of debts that get repaid first, and then the intensity of it reduces. So, you will pick the biggest debt to repay first, and then move to the next biggest, and then the next one, and so on!

Many debt experts call this technique the best one to adopt, as it gives the person many advantages. So if you have a lot of big debts to repay, then this is the best technique to employ, and not the other one. Let us now look at the various advantages and disadvantages of this technique.

Advantages

The main advantage of this technique is that, you will be done with a majority of your debts in no time at all! Once all your big debts have been repaid, you will only have to take care of the small ones, which are not really significant. So choosing this method is ideal for you and debt experts opine the same way. Another advantage is that, you won't have to take care of a big interest at the end of it. You will not have a large debt interest waiting for you and will only have a small interest to think of. So isn't that enough reason for you to pick this technique over the other?

Disadvantages

The main disadvantage of this technique is that, it will not do anything to increase your confidence. It will cause you to worry more as you will have to arrange for a big sum to repay the biggest debts. So you will have to come up with a large amount of money if you wish to use this technique. But once you do manage to raise the money, you will find it increasingly easy to repay the next biggest and then the next and so on. It is a matter of holding your nerve during the initial stages and not giving up on your debt repayment plans.

These are the two best techniques to employ and you can choose the one depending on your debt types.

As a word of advice, it is best to pool together all your debts and unify them. This will ensure that you pay towards just one source, as opposed to many different sources. You can unify it by borrowing the entire gamut from one source, such as a credit union, which will offer you a good interest rate. So say for example you owe A $5000 and B $3000. Both have asked for a 10% interest rate. You can approach a credit union for the $8000 and get it at a rate of 8%. This will ensure that you not only pay less but also have just one source to pay as opposed to two or three different creditors.

Step 3: Analyzing and Monitoring Your Budget

After you have successfully calculated your month on month income and expenses, you can now compare whether your budget creates a surplus or a deficit. If your monthly income surpasses your monthly expenses, you should encourage yourself and find a way to save or invest the additional income.

However, if your monthly expenses are greater than your monthly income, you should reconsider your budget and reduce some of the unnecessary expenses. If that nosedives, you can always increase your income by taking on a part time job or working overtime.

A budget is your path forward for spending and is a tool to help you attain your financial goals. Save your bills and take the time to combine all of your expenses for a month. Deduct your expenses from your Net Income. If the result is a positive number, then you are living within the limits of your regular income. If the result is a negative number, your expenditure is exceeding your income.

You need to question yourself, if each of this expense is a want or a need, and try to minimize spending on the wants. Most importantly, once you create a budget, stick with it. Make adjustments wherever necessary. Having a budget will allow you to control your money rather than your money controlling you.

In the previous chapter, we saw how it is possible for you to change up your budget and tweak it to leave you with a surplus. You must employ appropriate strategies to remain in surplus all through out and avoid having a deficit. Here are some things that you can do to cut down on the deficit and increase the surplus in a month.

- Is a particular expense item a "*need*" or a "*want*"? There is a clear line of difference between the two. A need is an absolute necessity and you simply cannot do without it. So it is compulsory that you undertake the process and not skip it. But a want is different. Man can want n number of things and end up splurging money unnecessarily. So cutting down on the wants is always a good plan as opposed to cutting down on a need. Go through your spending plan and check for both of these aspects as the first step to correcting your budget.

- Once you make the choice, bifurcate them accordingly. If it is a *need* are you getting the best value for your money on spending? You must make sure that you are not over paying for that particular item. A budget helps you to question and examine the cost and benefit of every expense you go through. This is very important, as you must know whether what you are paying is the right amount or if it is on the higher side. Even your needs can be over charged and it is up to you to decide whether or not you are paying the right amount for it. Don't think all your needs are important either and try to prioritize them. You will understand their true worth only if you cut loose some of the unnecessary needs that you might be catering to on a monthly basis.

- If the expense item is a *want*, you should ask if it is important in your lifestyle. If not, then try to eliminate it. If it is important, then again are you paying too much for the item? You may have fixed your mind on the item expense years ago not realizing that you can pay less for the same item today. Sometimes it is as easy as asking the item's provider to give you a better price or maybe look at a vendor who offers you for less. It pays to do a little research yourself and see if you are missing out on a good deal. All you have to do is go online and visit a comparison site. There, you will find the different deals that are available for you to choose from. Don't think you will not get a better deal than what you already have. You will definitely find it if you look in all the right places. You will only benefit from this activity so don't think of it as a tedious process. You cannot afford to be lethargic when it comes to your budget and must be ready to spring into action whenever need be.

- Is the expense item permanent or just temporary? Many expenses have a scope that is limited – kid's activities, education costs, car payments, mortgage, etc. Knowing the expense item's time frame can often help you to adjust your spending to ensure the most successful outcomes. Accept that financial and lifestyle circumstances change and your budget must be stretchy to adapt with those changes. The best thing to do to understand this better is writing down the temporary and permanent expenses in two different columns. That will help you see clearly what the different expenses are and whether or not they are really important.

- If there are certain expenses that you can skip in a month then you must do so by all means. This can be skipping a hobby class or some such. Don't worry; you can again rejoin the class in half a years time provided you have worked towards repaying your debts. You will be happy for having done the needful and begin to enjoy the class more when you take it up after the break. You can also set aside a fund for it and use it when it reaches the minimum amount required. Doing so will help take some of the weight off of your shoulders and you will also not have to miss taking part in activity that you like performing.

- Is the item a duplicated expense? For example, at your employment or privately, you may be paying for extended medical, dental and insurance benefits you already receive from your spouse's employer. Many expense decisions are made in seclusion of each other and, thus, you may end up paying for the expense twice. This is a little rare but possible nonetheless. Don't think you will not have such erroneous expenses in your budget. They will exist for sure and you have to look them up to fix them. Once you do spot them, make it a point to not repeat them the next time. You will realize that there are lesser mistakes in your spending habits once you start preparing the budget. So it is never a bad idea to start preparing one and make the most of the practice.

- Your home budget should be updated and reviewed at 4 times in a year to ensure that your expenses remain in line with the product and service benefits you are receiving. These 4 months is every quarter year. If you think your expenses are slightly over board, then you can review it every month if you like. Get into the habit of preparing a budget on a monthly basis and tell yourself that there are no two ways about it. Your budget will only make your life simpler and help you save oodles of money in a month.

- You must take these processes seriously and not assume them to fall into place by themselves. If you don't put in efforts to correct your errors then nobody else will do it for you. It will be a bit tough during the initial stages but you must stay put and do the best that you can to save money and not end up spending it all. Of course it will be tough during special occasions such as the birth of a child or your wedding but then too, you must do your best to save money instead of wasting it.

Step 4: Balancing Checkbook And Credit Cards

Keep a tab on your checkbook. The money balance in your checkbook is a serious number in money management because it permits you to know precisely how much money currently you have to save or spend. Keeping a precise checkbook register also allows you to review where you spend your money. Be sure to record all transactions, including ATM/Visa Check and Card transactions and deposits. Login to your account and check online.

Minimize the use of Credit Cards

Millions of Americans today are in debt. Credit card debt is an easy con to fall into. The best way to avoid this trap is by avoiding the usage of credit cards altogether. If you like the handiness of a credit card, consider getting a check card in place of it.

Check cards are recognized at most places that accept credit cards. The difference is that the expense is automatically subtracted from your checking account balance, which reduces your urge to spend more than you have. Be sure to keep a tab on each check card transaction in your checkbook ledger, just like you would do, if you wrote a check.

Cutting on Credit card usages

As you know, your credit cards are your worst enemies when it comes to repaying your loans. They will pull you down and make it impossible for you to increase your savings. Here are some things that you can do to reduce your credit card usage and cut it by half.

Before you go about these processes, start by understanding how much you end up paying using your cards in a month. You must look at all your expenses and see how much you pay using your card. Once you have the statistics with you, you will know how much damage your cards are really causing. The rate of interest will be supremely high and your cards will literally drain all you money from your accounts. But despite knowing this fact, more and more people still end up using their credit cards, and find themselves in a helpless position month after month. This exercise will pinch you hard and help you snap back to reality.

Return cards

The very first thing to do is return the cards that you have. I know that is tough to do but needs to be done at any cost. Choose cards that are new and return them one by one. It is very tempting to buy a new card as soon as the old one maxes out but you must control your urges. Start by returning your most recent card and then move to the next most recent one. But make sure the card does not have any credit when you are returning it. It will make it look like you have maxed out on it even if you have a lot of money on it. So leave only little in it and then return. But don't go on a rampage and spend all of it in one day. Go about it slowly and use your cards wisely before returning them.

Keep oldest

Whatever you do, don't surrender your oldest card. The basic idea is to hold on to the card that is having a great payment history. That will show well on your credit report and any financial institution will be happy to lend you a loan based on your report. But if you end up surrendering that card, then you will automatically cancel out all that history. That's a very big risk to take and it is best that you place your oldest or best card someplace safe.

Hide them

Many times, it will be impossible for you to give up on your cards owing to mental and emotional restrictions. But that is not reason enough for you to hold on to these cars and it is best to get rid of them some way or the other. You can do basic things like hiding it or asking a family member to hide it and not give away its location at any cost. You can also try freezing them, which means you can't access them without breaking the ice. These are extreme steps but are important, as you will not willingly give up on your cards if such drastic measures are not implemented.

Get small cards

The next time to visit the gas station or the department store, get yourself some small store cards. This will prevent you from using your credit cards at these places. When it is time to pay, you will only bust out your individual store cards and not feel the need to use your credit cards. But don't buy big cards that have a lot of value on them. They need to be of nominal values. Ask them for the smallest cards and use them regularly until they are completely used up and then renew them once more.

Get secured credit

The next novel idea is to get yourself a secured credit card. As the name suggests, this card is secured and is linked to your own savings account. But don't confuse it with a debit card. A debit card will not require you to add back the money you withdrew from your account by using it; on the other hand, a secured card will require you to add back the money into your account within a certain period of time. There is no interest here, which makes it a great option for you. But if you default on repaying the amount, then you will have to pay a fine.

Have a cash wallet

Maintain a cash wallet for yourself. It is understandable that you will not have the habit of withdrawing cash for yourself but it is important that you develop the habit before it's too late. Get yourself a nice big wallet that has no card slots in it. Withdraw a certain amount that will be enough for you to use on a daily basis. Carry the wallet around with you everywhere you go. Don't carry your card at all, and have a different wallet for it. That wallet should be your absolute last resort and must only be used if there is an emergency.

Use cash for everything

Make sure you use your cash for every type of payment, including big-ticket items. These items if purchased using card can invite a lot of interest, which is a bad thing. You can take a friend along with you when you wish to make a big purchase and ask them to prevent you from making use of your credit card to pay for it. You will be thankful for your decision. Another idea is to shop online and use online payment.

Reward!

Rewarding yourself for not having used your card is always a good idea. You will be happy for not having used your card and resisted the temptation. This reward can be a day at the spa or a nice meal for yourself. As long as it makes you happy, you can choose anything that pleases you. Just make sure the reward is enjoyed once in a while and don't make it a regular affair.

These are some of the important things that you can do to stop using your credit card so regularly. You must go about it at express speed if you wish to make the changes permanent.

Step 5: Debt, Savings And Credit – A Perfect Plan

The first thing you should work towards is to pay off your Debt. If you have Credit Card debt or other debts, pay the maximum to your highest interest rate debts first and the minimum on lower interest debts, which allows you to pay debts faster.

Establish a perfect savings plan

When you pay your monthly bills, write a check for yourself and put it in your savings account. If you get your paycheck deposited automatically, ask your employer about having a portion of your paycheck deposited to your savings account. Try to know your Credit History. Credit reporting agencies help you to collect data regarding your credit repayment history.

If your report shows that you are late paying bills, have maximized lines of credit, or have bankruptcies or other collection activities, this will negatively impact your ability to get credit.

If you find incorrect information in your credit report, contact the credit-reporting agency. They are required to investigate the information within 30 days and delete the information if it cannot be verified. Your rights are further described in the Fair Credit Reporting Act. It is important that you check for every small detail in the report including your name and also your address. Nothing should be wrong in your document and everything must be perfect.

When you set out to pay your debts and create savings for yourself, there are certain questions that you must ask and answer if you wish to be left with enough savings at the end of the month. Here are the different questions explained.

- What's important to you about money? This is a very basic question to ask and answer. Don't stick to standard thoughts and answer it in the best possible manner to convince yourself that your money is of extreme importance to you and you are not taking it casually.

- What would you like to achieve with your money? This is the next most important question to ask and answer. Is the money you have in your possession being put to good use? Are you doing justice to the money that you hold? What do you plan to attain out of your wealth possession.

- When you think about your money, what concerns, needs or feelings come to mind? Do you fear losing it or spending all of it on unnecessary things or are you confident of saving money on a monthly basis and directing it into all the right accounts. These are some of the issues that need to be addressed early on if you wish to do justice by your wealth assets.

- What are your interests? Do they involve money? Will you

be requiring some to fulfill your needs and ambitions? Will there be a time in the future when you will need money to undertake a major activity?

- Where would you like to be in 10-20-30 years? Will you have your own business established? Will you also own a house and have enough money saved up in the bank for yourself? Will you be independent or depend on someone for your financial resources?

- What do you spend money on? What is your main expense in a month? Is it a major expense or are there many minor ones? Do you know exactly where a majority of your expenses are concentrated?

- What are does your personal balance sheet look like? Do you have one to begin with? Are the assets and liabilities listed out correctly? Have you accounted for all your incomes and expenses?

- What are your assets (car, home) and what are your liabilities (mortgage, student loans, obligations)? Does the latter outweigh the former? Is everything in its rightful place?

These are just some of the questions that you must ask and answer if you wish to manage your wealth the right way.

Investment Perspective

The questions that were asked previously pertained to personal questions that you must ask yourself. Now, we will look at investment questions to ask and answer.

- Are you comfortable taking risk? This is the most important question to ask yourself. Any investment comes with a certain degree of risk attached to it. You must understand the risk and also understand whether or not you have the capacity to handle it. Not everyone will have it and it is important that you know for sure whether you can take part in a gamble.

- What would trigger a greater emotional feeling - seeing an investment appreciate or depreciate 20%? This is a very good question to ask yourself. Not everyone is built alike and they will react differently to different situations. Some will be over excited to see appreciation and not so excited to see depreciation but some will get over anxious when they see a sudden depreciation and not so excited with an appreciation. So you must understand where you lie.

- Do others look to you for insight and guidance? Are you seen as a good investor and do others approach you to seek advice? This is an important question to ask and answer and will reveal to you your true worth.

- Is the topic of money something you avoid or does it interest you? Do you leave a room when money matters are discussed or decide to stay back and contribute towards the conversation?

- Can you talk about money with family members easily? Or do you feel uncomfortable talking about it to someone? Is it fine for you to open up about all your incomes and expenses or do you feel the need to keep it private?

Your personal take

Here are some personal wealth related questions to ask and answer

- Do you want to be involved and understand the investment decision-making process or would you rather have everything be taken care for you? This really has nothing to do with efficiency. It's about having your investments taken care of by someone who is quite experienced and will lead you correctly.

- Do you have professional advice today from a lawyer, insurance agent or accountant? Have you already availed their services and are following in on their advice? Have they asked you to do certain things that are beneficial for your finances? Are you compensating them for their advice and services? These are some of the important questions to ask and answer.

- Has the professional experience been a good one? Have they done the needful and assisted you in your financial goals? Have you increased your wealth's potential by availing their help or the results are not too satisfactory?

- Do you currently have confidence in your financial plan? Do you think the plan is good enough for you to maximize your wealth's potential? Is it a good plan that helps you increase your savings in a month? Ask and answer these questions to know whether you are truly and thoroughly satisfied with your savings plans.

- Do You Understand Investment Risk? Are you aware of the risks that your investments bring along and have you accounted for them? Do you know that it is possible to lose a certain amount of your money when you invest in these businesses?

- Do you find yourself gravitating towards one type of investment asset class – such as cash, bonds, or stocks? Do you think these are the best and safest options and they will provide you with guaranteed and great returns?

- Would you know how to compare the riskiness of a single blue chip stock versus a diversified mutual fund of growth stocks? Will you undertake performing a comparative risk analysis?

So what's your plan and perfect strategy?

Creating a successful financial strategy begins with knowing the client. An advisor that knows what your requirements and status can develop a better strategy to strengthen areas of deficiency and take advantage of areas of strength. From this professional assessment, it is easy to determine what financial management strategies will be most effective.

Part of preparing a solid financial strategy is when you are able to withstand all conditions. That is, if the economy goes down,

- Do you own investments that perform well in that environment? Have you studied it enough to know that your investment is in a safe place where it is possible for you to maximize its wealth potential?

- If the investment environment improves, are you well positioned to take advantage of this? Are you invested to understand that the environment will keep changing and the face of your investment will follow suit?

These questions are asked and answered so that you understand whether or not your investments are in a safe place. Not all places are safe and you must pick the ones that will not be negatively affected by inflation and other such financial and political upheavals.

Diversify with a proper plan

The financial market place is vast; take advantage of it. Do not complicate a large number of investments with a diversified portfolio. For many investors, uninspiring results are caused by making investments in products and not fully understanding the risks. In a future chapter, we will look at some of the investments that you can make on both a short term and a long-term basis. There, you will have to read everything carefully and decide on the best plan of action to adopt. Don't get over excited and take up everything at the same time. Take it slow and ensure that you are capable of making the right decisions for yourself and your wealth.

Be alert and active

Make sure you are in solid financial shape. Losing the discipline of saving for goals or constantly breaking budget is just like going on the field without stretching. If facts change, try to change your thinking. Having a defensive financial strategy when your financial situation is looking better may not be maximizing your goals. Remain diligent when it comes to your financial activities. Don't panic if there is an upheaval, remain calm and sort it out in the easiest and best possible manner.

Here are the different investment options that you can choose for yourself.

Investment options

Short term option
Short-term investment options are those, which will yield a monetary benefit within a short amount of time. The time frame varies from investment to investment, but in general, anything that gives a result within a year's time can be seen as a short-

term investment. Let us look at some options for you to try out.

Intraday trading:

The very first type of short-term investment to consider is intra day trading. The stock market is a place where millions of people buy and sell stocks on a daily basis. It is possible for you to buy and sell on a daily basis as well. So within a day, you will buy stocks of a company and then sell it to earn a profit. But this type of investment comes with its fair share of risk, which you should be willing to undertake. You must first study the stock market and its functioning and only then can you take part in this form of trading.

Options:

The next type of trading is known as options. Options can last a week or two unlike intraday trading. Here, you will not have to fully buy a stock, or a financial security, and can only pay a small amount of money to reserve it. If the stock rises in value then you will benefit from it, as you will only have to pay what you had agreed upon. But if the stock's price falls then you have the option to refuse buying it. The choice is fully yours but you will lose the advance that you had paid for it.

Treasury notes:

Treasury notes are also known as bonds. These are securities that will help you increase your initial investment, as a certain amount of interest will be added to it. The government will collect your money and promise to return it back along with a certain interest amount attached to it. This therefore is a safe option to consider for your investment, as the government will attach its guarantee to it. When you plan to sell the bond in the market, you will avail a higher rate for it, which will be much more than what you had bought the bond for. You can avail a bond for 3 months, 6 months or 1 year.

Bank savings:

Saving your money in a bank is a good short-term investment. All banks will take your money and keep it safe for you. They will offer a rate of interest just like the government offers for a bond. The rate of interest differs from bank to bank. You must choose a bank that offers you the best rate of interest for you savings. Online accounts are said to be the best choices as they will not only provide you with a good rate of interest but also allow you to access your account from anywhere.

Foreign exchange:

Foreign exchange refers to foreign currencies. You can buy and sell foreign currencies. Just like you would buy and sell stocks in a day, you can buy and sell foreign currencies in the same way. Their value will differ over the course of the day and you can buy it when it is low and sell it when it is high to realize a profit from it.

Long term options

Just like the short-term investments, you can also avail long-term investments. These investments are to be held on for at least 5 years and no less. In the mean time, you cannot access your investments and must wait until your investment matures, before you can access and use your money. Let us look at the best long-term options for you in this chapter.

Business investments:

The very first and best form of long-term investment is known as business investments. There are many business types to choose from and you can pick the one that fits your situation the best. You can either start a business yourself or invest in someone-elses business. Both will help you turn your investment into a profit. But remember that it might take anywhere from 3 to 5 years for you to see a rise in your profit levels and you must remain patient all through out.

Stocks:

Just like short-term stocks, there are also long term stocks that you can choose. These long-term stocks are meant to give you dividends and are not chosen for their face value. You must choose companies that are well renowned and are known to pay good dividends on a regular basis. You can consult an expert to choose the best stocks for you and invest in them for at least 5 to 10 years.

Real estate:

Real estate investments are great long-term investment choices to consider for your money. When you invest in real estate, not only do you buy a property permanently for yourself but also have the chance to rent it out. The rent will make for your monthly income and the value of the property will steadily rise over the course of time. You can sell the property after 5 or 10 years and come into a big profit. Until such time, you can enjoy the property and stay in it if you like.

Gold/ jewelry:

Investing in gold and jewelry is another great long-term investment choice for you. Gold and other such precious metals are traded in the bullion market. These are extremely valuable and you can buy and sell them to arrive at a profit. Their value will keep increasing and decreasing during the course of the day and you must choose a time when the value is lowest. You must then hold the investment for 5 to 15 years and not sell it in between, as its value might not be realized in full capacity.

Mutual funds:

Mutual funds are long term investments that can be held for 5 or more years. When you invest in a mutual fund, the manager will diversify your investments and invest a little in several forms of securities. All of these securities will together contribute towards making your investment lucrative. You cannot access your investments in between and must wait it out before accessing it at once.

These form the various short term and long term investments that you can choose for yourself.

Step 6: Understanding Wealth Management Options

Strategies that have tax Advantage are numerous. These investment options are available to those who are able to spend time to take advantage of them. If you approach the right advisor they will carefully assess prior year tax filings to identify areas to consider, which can include education plans, executive compensation programs, and specialized benefit plans. The taxation policy differs from state to state and you must know how you can prevent paying up a large amount in the form of tax. There are many things that you can do to serve this purpose and end up paying less than minimum of what is required to be paid by you. But for that to happen, you must indulge in prior planning and understand the various things that can be done legally to prevent paying up large amounts of money towards your taxes.

Remember that wealth management is an important part of your financial planning. Your wealth is your biggest asset and something that needs to be evaluated from time to time. When you wish to use your wealth the right way, you have to consider doing many things for it. These include wealth transfer and wealth protection. These are not just random wealth related words and require you to put in efforts to understand both and use to your advantage. In this chapter, we will look at both of these in detail and tell you what you must do to work both of them in the right way.

Wealth Transfer

Everyone should take basic estate planning steps, such as naming property correctly, establishing substitute decision makers and drafting clear estate documents. Simple gifting strategies over the long term could be a powerful tool. For higher net worth individuals there are well-established options offered by various companies to thoughtfully avoid overpaying taxes in the future. You must plan everything in advance and ensure that there are no discrepancies.

Remember that wealth transfer is not an easy job and there are many things that you must look into for it to work well for you. You can avail the help of a qualified expert to give you all the best ideas that can be employed to transfer your wealth to all the right resources. This is especially important for high net worth individuals whose families are split up and each of your children is located in different parts of the country or world. If you do not assess your wealth and end up leaving behind a confused mass then the rightful heirs will find it very difficult to get their fair share.

But don't think of wealth transfer as a herculean task either. It is easy to understand and follow provided you know what needs to be done and how. You can borrow a plan of action from someone who has already done it and can also approach a bank or wealth management firm to help you with your wealth.

Wealth Protection

A wealth management plan should have a full evaluation of liability exposure in all core areas. Extra insurance in many cases is warranted. You should consider expert opinion and adopt behaviors and strategies that avoid, prevent, reduce and transfer risk. A great deal of innovation has happened in life insurance over the years, which can offer a stable financial reserve for difficult times.

The very first thing you must do is buy an insurance policy that covers your new net worth. So say for example you are to receive a million dollars from your father as your inheritance. You must call your insurance company and tell them to give you a million dollar personal liability coverage. This will ensure that you have enough insurance for yourself and do not have to worry about your personal wealth protection. You can either get it done once the money actually comes into your account or can also do it just before it comes to you. Your wealth potential should be estimated and you must work towards protecting it at any cost.

Another important wealth protection activity involves checking all your joint accounts. These accounts can be jointly held with any person in your life including a sibling or a spouse. You must ensure that any activity taking place in that account has been approved by you and there are no suspicious withdrawals from it. These types of accounts are very risky to have with your partner as a divorce can spell doom and if the other person files first then you will end up losing the money to them. So consider all of this carefully before opening a joint account.

If you own a small company, then it is important that you buy a protective umbrella for that as well. Value your company and buy yourself proper insurance. One advantage of owning a sole proprietary business is that you don't have to worry about your partner's actions against the wealth of the company but you must be well aware that your company will be solely your responsibility and any expenses arising out of suing you will have to be borne by you.

If you have a partnership company, then make sure all the terms and conditions in regard to your company are sorted out clearly and there are no discrepancies. Everything should be well understood and sorted out if you wish to protect your wealth and the company's assets. These are very small actions to employ but will have a big impact on your business.

The more the measures you employ the better prepared that you are to protect your wealth. Try to think ahead of time and do all the right things in terms of your wealth management and wealth protection.

Working towards Charity

Charitable giving can bring significant meaning to the lives of those who receive, and offer, the donations. These should be thoughtfully considered and funded. Many people fail to have an action plan in place and end up either spending more or spending less than what they are supposed to. When you plan to give away money to charity, work with a blue print. You can formulate one depending on how much surplus you are left at the end of the month. If you start out during the start of the month, you will end up paying up throughout the course of the month. So make it a point to not go about it without a plan and ensure that you are prepared in advance to give away only a certain agreed upon amount to any charity or charities of your choice.

Your wealth needs to be managed and protected in the best way, if you wish to lead a stress free life. If it is over complicated then you will unnecessarily worry about it and not know if you are doing the right thing. So keep it simple and easy to follow. Once you understand how something works, it will get progressively easier. If you are on the verge of inheriting a large amount of money then it is best to remain prepared and avoid a "deer in headlights" situation.

Step 7: Engaging Wealth Management Experts

As we saw in the previous chapter, it is extremely important for you to manage your wealth and ensure that it is protected. Protecting your wealth is not only important for you but also for your family members and those that are part of your business. But it is next to impossible to do everything by yourself and you must employ a professional to help you out. These professionals are trained to help individuals manage their wealth and it is best to contact them when you wish to manage or protect your wealth. Start by choosing someone that is well renowned for the service he or she provides. These wealth mangers can either be found online or you can approach a bank to help you out. You can look up testimonials provided for them and choose someone you think is the best fit.

Once you do find one, you must adopt the following steps.

Phase I

Getting to know an advisor should be a deliberate & substantive process. You will receive real help as a potential client and these firms facilitate you to form a decision with a preliminary wealth management plan. This plan is arrived after information is received in the initial discovery meeting. Choose someone who stays close to your place so that you don't have to travel long distances to meet them. You can simply drive down and meet them within a few minutes and start your discussion as soon as possible. But if you think the best one stays far then make sure you reach their office on time and not end up canceling the meeting. Remain motivated enough to meet them when they ask you to come over and don't make it an ego game. Remember that managing your wealth is of utmost importance and it is best that you do everything in your power to manage it the right way. You must provide your manager with all the information that is requisite, and not hold back on anything. It is crucial that the person know exactly what your assets look like in order to help you plan and manage it.

Investment Plan

This is a substantive client specific document that takes several hours to prepare and present. It consists of a business objective analysis; employee characteristics and survey of plan options. When you are planning for wealth management options, making the right kind of documentation is extremely important and getting this done through experts makes lot of sense. Your wealth manager will help you come up with a plan of action for your investments. This plan must incorporate all the necessary investments that you will be making and how you plan to protect your wealth. It is understandable that you will have certain trust issues but that should not prevent you from doing the needful for your wealth. After a few sessions, you will begin to realize the true worth of your meetings with your manager and why it was a great decision for you to have a manager help you with your wealth management.

Mutual Commitment

After reviewing the retirement plan which has been mutually agreed upon for managing your wealth, you will have time to decide if you would like to go forward with that particular wealth management agency or not. So make the right move. Don't be in a hurry to come to a conclusion and take your time with it. You will have at least a month to decide upon the next course of action and so, take your time to decide whether what has been presented to you is the best option for you or you would like to make certain changes in it. Whatever you decide, it is best that you consult another expert for a second opinion on the matter. This person can be a friend who is already having his or her wealth managed and has availed retirement plans. But don't blindly trust their opinion either and have your own opinion as you are doing it for yourself.

Phase II

This is the phase were formal documents are signed. After a formal engagement letter being signed, the wealth management agency you are working with will write a detailed Investment Policy Statement & Implementation Plan for you. This plan becomes the basis for tracking progress and growth of your wealth. Be present all through out the process and avoid leaving town. You will be required to go through all the policies and their terms and conditions. Make sure you understand everything that there is to before signing on the dotted line. Once everything is done, refer to it once again to ensure that everything is correct and there are no errors anywhere. If there are, then get it rectifies at the earliest instead of wasting time. This phase is slightly more important than the previous one and will require you to be diligent.

Once everything is sorted out, it is best that you choose to indulge in regular follow-ups. Just because something is finished does not mean you not go through it again.

Key highlights

Busting the different myths that surround budgeting is the first activity that you need to take up. These myths will be majorly responsible for your pre formed opinions on the topic of budgeting, and it is important that you separate the facts from fiction. In the first chapter, we looked at all the important myths that surround budgeting and it is best that you go through it again to understand why budgeting is a great activity to take up and exploit.

It will be a bit difficult to take the process of budgeting seriously but you will have to spend some time understanding its true worth and putting in efforts to follow a strict schedule that will help you remain motivated and interested in it. Think of it as a fun activity that will help you save a lot of money. You must also get your spouse to join in and prepare a budget for themselves.

Next up, you must understand the various sources of income that will provide you with consistent money all through the month. The basic sources include your salary, which your employer will pay you and passive incomes that you will receive from all your passive activities. The third type of income is known as portfolio incomes, which you will receive from all your investments. All of these will collectively form your monthly income.

But this income will not suffice, and you must strive to earn a little extra every month. You can do so by taking up parallel activities that will allow you to remain with a little extra money at the end of every month. What you choose will depend on your hobbies and interests. You can also keep your options flexible and try out different activities to zero in on the best one for your talents and time.

The next thing to do is understand your monthly expenses. You will have a lot of expenses to take care of in a month and it is important that you make a note of all of them. Some of the basic expenses include gas, medical, groceries, telephone bills and electricity bills. All of these are to be taken care of if you wish to avail uninterrupted service.

Formulating the budget refers to preparing your monthly budget, which incorporates your net incomes and expenses. You must choose a simple format for yourself and fill in the details one after the other. We looked at a sample in the book that you can choose and follow for yourself. Remember that the same format will not work for everyone and you must choose something that works best for you.

Correcting your budget is extremely important. It is not necessary that you will always be left with a surplus. You might also be left with a deficit, which will have to be fixed. You can fix it by correcting your budget and decreasing your expenses to first match the incomes and then reducing it further to be left with a surplus. This surplus can then be invested in short term or long-term investments. You will have to decide on the best amounts that can be directed into these individual accounts.

Credit cards are your biggest enemies when it comes to saving money for your future. You have to learn to use them judiciously and not pay extreme interests. You can also undertake extreme steps such as cutting or shredding your cards so that you don't feel tempted to use them at all. Just remember to hold on to the oldest card that you own, as it will have a good record history. Maintain a cash wallet that you can carry everywhere with you and also use your cash to purchase big ticket items. Carry a friend with you when you go shopping to help you stay away from your card.

Debt repayment strategies are aplenty and you must choose one that works best for you. Although both the snowballing and the avalanche method are recommended, you must choose it carefully. Both come with their due pros and cons and you must pick the one that fits your debt type the best. You can avail the assistance of a qualified accountant to help you out. You must do your best to repay all your debts within the earliest possible time, and not wait for the interest to build up for a long time.

Wealth management is an important topic to address. When you have a large amount of wealth to look after, it is advisable to take the help of an expert. This expert can be a wealth manager, who will take all your information and come up with a proper wealth management strategy for you. You must work closely with them and take the next step only if you like what they have proposed for your investments. Remember that the final nod should come from you alone and until such time, your money cannot be touched by anyone.

Investment options are plenty and you must choose the one that suits your needs the best. Right from short term to long-term investments, there are many options such as intraday trading and mutual fund investments, and each one comes with its own set of pros and cons. So you must choose the one that provides you with better returns and reduces your risk considerably. Here too, you must avail the help of an expert and choose an investment that will increase your wealth potential.

Conclusion

An individual's financial obligations towards his/her creditors are known as liabilities. Liabilities can range from credit card debt to personal loans. While computing your total liabilities, keep in mind to include every possible liability irrespective of its economic importance. Student loans, mortgage, medical bills, collection accounts and credit card balances can all be classified as liabilities.

In the past, if you have co-signed a loan for someone else, be sure to include this loan as one of your liabilities. The reason behind this is quite simple, if the other person skips and vanishes, you are legally obligated to repay that loan.

After writing down all your assets and liabilities on a piece of paper, you can compute your net worth by deducting your total liabilities from your total assets. If the computing yields a positive number, your overall financial state is in good condition. If the result shows a negative value, do your best to decrease your debt while increasing your assets.

If your net worth is dangerously negative, you might be insolvent and would have to act quickly to get your finances back on the right track. If you are unable to do so, you may be forced to file for bankruptcy to ease some of those high debt amounts.

In any case, make sure that you turn positive and always try to stabilize your financial situation. I want to thank you for choosing this book and hope you find it informative.

www.ingramcontent.com/pod-product-compliance
Lightning Source LLC
Chambersburg PA
CBHW071609170526
45166CB00003B/1035